SEVEN SECONDS

Free Thoughts of a Psychotherapist

www.dorakiki.com

London.uk

Publisher ©2021 Dora & Kiki Ltd

Author ©2021 Oscar Travino

Illustrations ©2021 Various Authors

ALL RIGHTS RESERVED

© Copyright 2021 - All rights reserved.

The content contained within this book may not be reproduced, duplicated or transmitted without direct written permission from the author or the publisher.

Under no circumstances will any blame or legal responsibility be held against the publisher, or author, for any damages, reparation, or monetary loss due to the information contained within this book. Either directly or indirectly.

Legal Notice:

This book is copyright protected. This book is only for personal use. You cannot amend, distribute, sell, use, quote or paraphrase any part, or the content within this book, without the consent of the author or publisher.

Disclaimer Notice:

Please note the information contained within this document is for educational and entertainment purposes only. All effort has been executed to present accurate, up to date, and reliable, complete information. No warranties of any kind are declared or implied. Readers acknowledge that the author is not engaging in the rendering of legal, financial, medical or professional advice. The content within this book has been derived from various sources. Please consult a licensed professional before attempting any techniques outlined in this book.

By reading this document, the reader agrees that under no circumstances is the author responsible for any losses, direct or indirect, which are incurred as a result of the use of information contained within this document, including, but not limited to, errors, omissions, or inaccuracies.

Seven Seconds

Table Of Contents

CHAPTER I GALLIPOLI, SUMMER 2017 5
CHAPTER II INSPIRATION 9
   THE DISEASE OF THE ELSEWHERE 9
   RESPONSIBILITY 14
CHAPTER III. PAUSE 17
CHAPTER IV EXHALATION 23
   LETTING GO TO EMBRACE 23
CHAPTER V. BEYOND THE VEIL OF FEAR 29
   BEYOND ANY CERTAINTY 29
CHAPTER VI YOU AND I 35
   ONE, TWO, THREE 36
   HUMANE, TOO HUMANE 39
   AN HOUR, A DAY, OR A LIFETIME 41
CHAPTER VII OF WATER AND WIND 47
   FORGET YESTERDAY, START TODAY 54
CHAPTER VIII I START AGAIN FROM MYSELF 55
   "KNOW YOURSELF" 55
   #COMMUNICATING? 57
   IT HAPPENED ON THIS DAY 59
CHAPTER IX CUM-FINIS 67
   CONFINES 67
   IDENTICAL AND DIFFERENT 71
   "IT'S NOT EASY" 83
   "IF YOU ARE NICE, I LOVE YOU" 87
   "HOME IS WHERE YOU ARE" 88
   "TRUTH IS PROTECTION" 89
   WHAT IF LEAVING MEANT GOING BACK? 91
   FEELING, NOT THINKING 93
   25TH DECEMBER 95
CHAPTER X AND I SMILE AT MY NOW 101
   I CHOOSE TO BE 104

Seven Seconds

Chapter I
Gallipoli, Summer 2017

I go back there, where it all began.

Because every circle closes.

Here, on this cliff that inspired so many of those free thoughts that took form in my first book, Now or Never.

It's the same sunset,

but it's a different sunset.

It's the same me,

but it's a different me.

Two years ago,

this moment.

I relax my muscles on the bare rock.

The sea is calm today.

No noise in the air apart from the wind.

And I smile at my Now.

To those who wear Now,

and keep playing

Only the ideas we actually live are of any value.

[Hermann Hesse]

Seven seconds. It is the time for a full and deep breath. Inhale, pause, exhale.

A breath.

Seven seconds, those that report the crossroads of the most important moments of your life.

Breathe in.

Close your eyes, drop your thoughts, and listen. Exhale, and take that first step.

Cogito ergo sum

[Descartes]

No, it is not.

It is not true that you always have to think about it.

It is not true that reasoning will solve any doubt or fear for you.

It's not true. Rather.

I made some of the most important decisions of my life by blocking the flow of an unstoppable whirlwind of thoughts that only bridle me in a web of inextricable fears.

I closed my eyes for a moment.

I felt a point here, suspended between my stomach and my throat.

I took a deep breath, opened my eyes, and took the first step.

And I let myself go, with confidence, to the inescapable flow of our Becoming.

Sometimes the answer is to block each question.

Indulge in something greater.

Trust the flow of life.

Simply feel.

Spiro ergo sum.

I breathe, so I am.

Seven Seconds

Chapter II
Inspiration

The Disease of the Elsewhere

Think about it. We are all sick, with a subtle and persistent disease. A muted disease that apparently makes no noise. I call it the disease of the elsewhere.

We are always in an indefinite elsewhere; another time, another place, other people. At the table, with friends, we are on our cell phones to write to another friend (and then, when we are with that friend, maybe we write to someone else).

We relate our time to a bygone time. —It was better before—, —when I was younger—, —if only I had—, —who knows what it would have been like—. Otherwise, we are in future projections. The commitments of the next day, the worries about work, the stressed and persistent expectation of happiness postponed, always, to a moment to come. When I get the car, When I get my degree, When I get the job, When I'm in a relationship, When I have a home, When I have children.

Then, inevitably, we move to a further elsewhere when we have obtained them. This is how we crush and mortify our time, our life, the breath of our Now. A—today—that loses energy and enthusiasm every day.

There!

It is an excellent way to make yourself unhappy, delegating expectations to space—beyond—that has the consistency of pure thought. Tomorrow does not exist. It will be a new today in 24 hours. And today will be what you tomorrow call yesterday. You will look at it with nostalgic regret and say, "if only I had...", "who knows what it would be like if..." So?

Do you still want to fool yourself, getting lost in the maze of elsewhere and lost possibilities, or do you choose to act today?

Wherever you are, you really have to be there. Each moment is unique and will never come back. It is your time, your life. And it is Now.

We live in a historical era characterized by a sort of psychopathology of the—elsewhere—. Just look around to catch the signs. Groups of friends at the café tables, each busy on their mobile phones. The seated body, an uninhabited shell. The mind, who knows where. The worker, at the end of his day, walks the road that leads him home. He goes through a park with benches, trees, and children playing. He does not see them. His thoughts are already about the next day; an important business meeting awaits him, and he is worried.

An acquaintance of mine, he is about 40 years old, lives every day the anguish linked to the thought of when his parents will die. He says he already knows that he won't be able to make it without their presence. His parents are in perfect health today. A young girl walks with her girlfriends on the pier. It is a beautiful sunny spring day. Someone has decided to lie down to enjoy that first warmth. She does not look around her, but inside herself, in memories that break her smile and her breath; in that place, a year ago, she was with her ex-boyfriend, for whom she still suffers. A young working mom does everything in a rush. From her awakening, she experiences a sort of competition with herself to fit her commitments. She arrives at the end of the day exhausted, and she still does not stop; she is already thinking about her next day's commitments. Our mind is full of things that risk becoming garbage. Residuals of ancient fears, past experiences from which we still allow ourselves to be held back today, future projections, worries and expectations, old grudges and regrets of situations never lived.

The energy that disperses. Action that stops. An immense, colossal devaluation of one's present. This Now that configures as the only space-time in which all our power to change is concentrated and that too often we crush and trample. It is time to go back to yourself, to your breath, to your really being there. Here, now. Homecoming is the essential basis for really feeling and allowing the self to let its real needs emerge.

Stop.

Breathe.

Not—cogito ergo sum—but—I breathe; therefore, I am—.My body, my feelings, these hands that grab, and these steps that I can move. In my body.

I live it, and I feel at home.

I will set out on the road.

It always leads to another dawn.

[Kahlil Gibran]

You've been through a lot, that's true. Disappointments, errors, falls, and hesitations, abandonments, emptiness, loneliness, and silence. But you are here, right now. Still and forever, you breathe and exist. Folded silently to count your wounds like the vertebrae of your back. One on top of the other, to draw the profile of your being a Woman. The backbone of your being in the world, built step by step on your story. One sudden movement and you're back on your feet. Dry your eyes girl, no pain is forever. Everything changes in this world, even your emotions, if you allow yourself to experience them. Your every tear will return new light to your eyes, held in the folds of an excited smile. There will always be new dawn at the end of each night. Life is like this, marvelous in its surprise. Take a step. It will change; it is already changing. Because—always—is never, and—never—is still and always.

Our heads are round

so our thoughts can change direction

[Francis Picabia]

It's time to take your time. It's time to ask yourself if this is the life you want and how much you are choosing it. It's time to get back to you, to live according to your values. We build too many castrating cages. Or we accept them as an immutable part. —Because it is like this—, —because I am born this way—, —because it is what others expect—.

Freedom.

We look for her, but she frightens us. Because being free means that you alone are responsible for what you choose, do, and the life you lead. So better choose a guilty part. An enemy to which attribute our miseries.

Happiness breaks the rules. It is jump, it is courage, it is disobedience.

Responsibility

From the Latin—*respòndere*—, —*to be responsible for somebody*—, (and oneself) about one's actions. In Gestalt therapy, it is understood as *response-ability*, that is, the ability to respond to an event, to overcome discomfort, to develop the ability to respond adequately to a situation. It is a practice of awareness to direct our energies into the present and the experience of contact with others in the Here and Now, the only dimension in which the human being has power.

It is the only way to connect with life, give objective and subjective meaning to our existence in the world. Maybe we should rediscover the direct thread of our feelings. No more subliminal messages on Facebook, no more tactics of silence, no more anger, no more not expressed emotions. If you are angry, be angry. If you are sad, go ahead and cry. If you love that person, tell them. Let's take responsibility for our emotions.

What are you doing for yourself? Maybe you work, fix up the house, take your children to school, cook. Maybe you go to the beautician, buy a pair of shoes, go shopping. Maybe you go on a diet, maybe to the gym. Maybe you buy a new dress or a new lipstick. But you know, you are certainly not just a body. You are certainly not just your appearance.

What are you doing for yourself? Do you take care of your thoughts and emotions? Do you ever stop and wonder if you live the life you want? Do you ever walk barefoot on the grass, looking at the clouds in the sky? Do you look at the world you live in, or have you stopped exploring and discovering? Do you laugh? Do you still get excited, or do you run between the folds of your commitments until the evening, exhausted, and then start over? Life is not a race. The only destination is the center of oneself. If there is a goal, it is; to become who you are.

Because the world is beautiful, girl. It is you who insist on looking at it only from the same side. Change perspective, open your eyes, use your senses. There are lands to discover and perfumes to be smelled. You have heart, come on!

Someone's sitting in the shade today
because someone planted a tree a long time ago.
[Warren Buffett]

Look, it's not true that there is only one way of being in the world.

In the end, do you think other people's approval matters more than your happiness?

Make every action entail new paths. New paths entail growth, and growth involves new possibilities.

Everything starts with something or someone. Every trip, every work, every business. And then that gesture expands, like the voice in a choir or the smell of coffee in a house. Light calls the light, and a first step will move another hundred.

Start now.

You were born free. And for how much rain you have gone through, your wings are there, still and always ready to support your flight.

Be true to yourself before others. Do the things you want. Rationalize your fears; you don't take these risks after all.

Get rid of the judgment of others; it is the main obstacle to your shine. No one is perfect; we are human beings, and we are beautiful for that. Like yourself, you don't have to be well-behaved but genuine.

Because every day comes to an end, and when the light goes down, you will be alone, a spectator and judge of your choices.

Only a judge will be there at the end of our time, "Did I live the life I wanted?"Choose your way, choose your path.

It's *your* life, do it as *you* wish.

Chapter III.
Pause

Indifference is the dead weight of history

[A. Gramsci]

This is how it starts. With a gesture of renunciation justified as laziness and carelessness. Something like—oh well... Oh well.

It is said that if you place a live frog in a pan of cold water on the fire, it will continue to croak candidly. She does not try to run away, ignoring the progressive rise in temperature, until she finds herself dead, burned. Ignoring, letting go, is the substratum on which abuses, violence, oppression, mafias, degradation arise. A gesture of carelessness cannot be unconscious.

Never.

We choose it, perhaps with a non—choice.

We do a lot to complain about what we don't like, and then we end up devaluing what we have to do something and change.

But—oh well...

Oh well, it's just a possibility. Oh well, it is only this time. Oh well, someone else. Oh well, nothing is going to happen anyway. Oh well, it is useless. Oh well, it's late.

—Oh well—is the beginning of the end of any possibility of a better life. The self—proclaimed silence for your space. The self—evaluation of all your powers. Because if you don't care about today, there will be no tomorrow.

If you want things to change, start changing things.

Neglect is the basis of degradation. One feels as though authorized to no longer have attention for oneself and others. A broken window involves another glass break, in a spiral of urban and social decay (as claimed by the theory of broken windows by J. Q. Wilson and G. L. Kelling). The same goes for your home, for your couple, for your person. Every act of carelessness is a piece you add to a mosaic of mortifying decay.

Never underestimate it.

It got late so soon.

[Dr. Seuss]

What is all this fury for the—late—?

You came late.

Now it's late.

I'm late.

I realized it late.

Nobody ever cares about—early—.

Being early.

Skipping steps.

Wanting everything at once.

Anticipating the work, the fears, the whole life.

—Early—has the same connotation as—late—.

You're out of time, anyway.

There is only one right time; this moment.

Your present, and your desire to live it, with confidence, energy, and full awareness.

The past is behind us.

The future is desire and guidance.

The present is your open hands, your breath, and your ability to let go.

Come on.

Start with you, start with a gesture.

An act of love, whatever it may be, can be the basis for the construction of new scenarios.

Love for you, for others, for the spaces you live, for what you do, for your dreams, for the things you believe in.

A small gesture expands. Spreads. It radiates.

Like a smile, like a caress, like the scent of coffee in a house. Get started now. Take care of what's important to you. *It's your life; give it the love you deserve.*

Choosing always means taking something but giving up something else. For heaven's sake, we can always go back if we realize that the path chosen is no longer for us. There is no fault or defeat in this. But perhaps that is why choosing is so difficult for some. The non-choice allows us to stay in the muffled limbo of open possibilities. But be careful. Because in the world of—everything is possible—, we risk making nothing possible. And yet, let's think about how many times we end up doing it, shifting responsibility and possibility out of ourselves, on the outside, onto someone else. A perfect way to deprive ourselves of any possibility of intervention and remain in a victim position, where power is delegated to others.

A lack of responsibility is also a profound self—depreciation. Let's stop saying—I can't—, let's stop complaining. This position cannot hold up forever, and sooner or later, we will find ourselves dealing with—if only I had...So? What do you choose today?

—Courage—. From cor, cordis, —heart—

and habere, —to have—.

Literally to have heart.

And as long as that heart beats,

a choice is always possible.

[The now or never]

Do you know that someday nothing will hurt more than regret?

B. Wire, an American nurse of terminal patients, has collected their testaments in a book. The title, direct, is "I wish I had." The leading source of suffering, at the end of this life, is regret for what has not been. Whoever is at the end of his days, deeply relativizes the fears and blocks that for so much of life have prevented the realization of desires and dreams. That fear, in that last moment, finally appears for what it is; a self-imposed mental fence, dissolving in the face of the awareness only when the heart stops beating, too late. Perhaps even today, you look back and, of those regrets, you feel that you have accumulated a lot of them. What is certain is that looking back will not take back time. What has been, has been. But now imagine yourself in 5 or 10 years. What new regrets do you think you will have that day?

Here it is. Stop. Take a moment, and think hard about it. All of this is not there yet, but there is still your chance to determine it or not.

If we wait for the moment when everything,

absolutely everything is ready,

we shall never begin.

[I. Turgenev]

No reasoning will give you the correct answer. Living is also and above all experimenting, trying, getting involved. Between doing and not doing, choose the doing. And, if you try and fail, you still learn something. It is allowed to make mistakes, do you know? Life is not meant to be thought. It is made to be lived. Not doing, for fear of making a mistake, means having already made a mistake. And nothing is more terrible than a thought that silently comes to mind; —if only I had... So? If not now, when?

Chapter IV
Exhalation

Letting Go to Embrace

Forgiveness does not mean canceling a wrong suffered. It is a process that does not condone anyone but frees those who decide to embrace it. Forgiveness means releasing one's negative energies still tied to something or someone. Energies that, in fact, keep us bound in a spiral of continuous frustration and self—torment. If you forgive, it is for yourself. Because you feel you deserve something other than a mortified present imprisoned in webs of resentment. So you choose to feel the earth under your feet and the freedom to move and walk in your today. Walking your way with a light step and with the fullness of your breath.

Letting go does not mean forgetting. It means choosing to accept that things went a certain way. Non—acceptance binds us and consumes us with anger and resentment. Letting go means looking at your today. It is not an amnesty to the other but a gift to oneself.

A gesture of grace and respect towards one's world and one's well-being.

Deciding always means taking something but giving up something else. The verb to decide comes from the etymology—to cut away—. The words murder and suicide come from the same etymology. A decision embraces one possibility and —kills—another. Perhaps this is why choosing is so difficult for many.

The non—choice allows us to remain in the muffled limbo of open possibilities. It is like saying it is better to string along into the thought of—I wonder how would it have been like if...—, rather than facing the courage of a position. But be careful. Because in the world of—everything is possible—, we risk making nothing possible.

Try, dare, launch yourself, make mistakes, fall, get up, try again, live! Everything that today blocks you in a web of fears has the consistency of pure thought. You built it, day after day. And day after day, you can choose to stop listening to it. So come on, choose to live. One day you will think about it with a smile, and you will say that yes, it was worth it. You did what was right with your life; you really lived it.

And in today already walks tomorrow.

[Samuel T. Coleridge]

Do you know what the mistake is? You over-invest the future. Or allow the past to hold you back. But the past is gone, and the future is just an idea built on the present. A present to which you keep stubbornly saying—no— because you don't live it, because you are afraid, because you expect a mortgage on your future (Will it be okay? Will it be worth it? Will I regret it? Is it the right choice?) that, after all, you know it well, nothing and nobody can give to you. In life, you know as much as I do that there are no guarantees. But a guarantee is instead the ability to truly live today. Completely. And many have really lived today who create their own history and their own tomorrow.

My dream is fed with abandonment, with regret.

I love only the roses that I did not pick.

I love only things that could have been and haven't been.

[Guido Gozzano]

Too much life spent navigating the waves of lost possibilities. Hints of regret to cloud the transparency of your today. But life not lived is not the life you haven't lived.

Simply... it's not.

It is an idealization. Something that has the consistency of a fairy castle, like the ones in the fairy tales you listened to as a child.

And the reality of your days cannot be compared with a pure idea. They are not made of the same matter.

The time spent navigating the folds of the unlived is just time you waste. It is the life you take away.

Look.

You have your hands and your thoughts.

You have your eyes and your words.

You have your legs and this moment.

And if this life isn't what you want, then move on and start changing it.

That's life. Yours, the only one you have.

And all that is given to you is to ensure that it is truly lived.

The chief danger in life is that you may take too many precautions

[A. Adler]

Do not fool yourself. Your idea that you can control everything is just a lie. And too often, it is the excess of control that causes you to lose control.

You don't control events, tides, seasons, the autonomic nervous system, and you can't control your emotions.

The world changes.

It is not the change itself that creates suffering but your resistance to it.

It is a bit like driving a dam in a torrent of water; tension is created, a resistance.

And that is the leading cause of your suffering.

In so much of your life, the flow together with the change would bring the balance back to its natural essence.

Stop resisting, and become an integral part of the river, of the natural becoming of all things.

Let things happen.

Live them, feel them. Move with not against things.

Learn to loosen your grip and allow your fingers to caress the change.

Abandon yourself.

There are things, whether you like it or not, that just happens.

A sudden smile happens.

The unexpected happens.

Your changing body happens.

A ray of sunshine happens on a gloomy day.

It happens to fall in love.

A flower happens between the tracks of an old station.

A meeting happens, an end happens, and a new beginning happens.

Stop resisting.

Open your arms to change. Breathe it.

That's life. Magnificent and alive in its always knowing how to surprise you.

Chapter V.
Beyond the Veil of Fear

Beyond any Certainty

Do you know what your *comfort zone* is?

It is the perimeter within which you circumscribe your life; the same people, habits, roles, the same dynamics. Maybe you complain about it, perhaps they don't satisfy you, yet you keep choosing them. You choose them for a ridiculous and easy reason; they make you feel safe because you know them, and in this way, you prevent yourself from meeting an unknown who scares you.

The comfort zone is a golden cage. It is the reassuring embrace of a mother, the muffled and warm passage of hours or whole life. Hot. Comfortable. But there is no growth, no evolution.

Growth is embracing the unknown. Growth is exploring new roles and new parts of oneself. Growth is getting away from the mother's arms and exploring the world, exploring oneself. You have parts of you that are there in the shadows. Fallen asleep for years of—always all the same—. Pull them out, explore, surprise yourself again.

Take the risk of really living.

Or is it evil what we fear,

or the damage is that we are afraid

[Sant'Agostino]

—Fear of being trapped in traffic —, —knowing you have a way out—, —getting out immediately—, —knowing you can go home—.

These are the phrases I often hear from people who suffer from anxiety and panic attacks.—Knowing you can go home—.Here it is.

There is a fundamental perceptual error in this mindset.

Because—Home—is and must be our body,

our breath, our feeling.

The center of us, wherever we are.

It is clear that if the body ceases to be home, home is nowhere. There is no place. It is not possible to escape from oneself.

To really go home safe means to regain the most authentic and profound contact with your center. Fear, like other emotions, has a fundamental adaptive function; it allows us to recognize danger and cope with it.

It is due to the emotion of fear that, over millennia, we have been able to avoid ferocious beasts, defend ourselves from attacks, avoid dangerous situations, survive in conditions where attack or getaway constituted the borderline between life and death. But, for fear to make sense, there must be a danger. Or it all comes down to a mortifying castle of pure paralyzing fantasies.

Fear of public speaking.

Fear of taking an exam.

Fear of expressing one's opinion.

Fear of experiencing a new part of oneself.

Always ask ourselves if we are in *real* danger.

Let's reduce our fears before our fears reduce us.

I postpone death by living,

 by suffering, by error, by risking, by living, by losing.

[Anaïs Nin]

The fear of making mistakes is one of the primary limits to express what you are or may become.

Fear of not being appreciated, of not being loved anymore, of being judged, of making mistakes.

On closer inspection, these are fears related to our childish side, when preserving the love of one's parents was the fine line between living or imagining dying.

It is devastating for a child to imagine that he is no longer loved by his attachment figures.

So better be—good—or better be what others expect from us.

But today?

Today you are an adult, and the essence of who you are is certainly not tied to the opinion of others.

And, whether you like it or not, everyone will never like you, whatever you are.

So come on. Living is also courage, letting go of what still keeps us anchored to old patterns and embracing fuller ways of being in the world.

Because, as R. L. Stevenson writes, if there is a purpose in life, it is to be what we are, to become what we are capable of becoming.

Finally free to really be ourselves.

Avoiding abandoning yourself to love for fear that it may end means precluding you from being happy Now. And—now—is all you have.

There is no lifetime warranty for anything.

It would be like not enjoying the breeze of dawn on a summer morning because, inevitably, the day will turn its back as night falls.

But the night will then end.

And there will always, always, be a new day to caress your eyes.

We use incredible strategies to avoid taking responsibility for our life.

Even reaching the point of being unhappy, victimizing ourselves, identifying enemies, and blaming ourselves for our miseries.

A change is often a change of perspective.

It happens when you realize that external enemies are nothing but images that you created for not seeing how little courage you thought you had.

But courage is a prerogative of being alive. It is an integral part of your heartbeat. Happiness is a leap into the void,

but the place you fall into is in the center of you.

"And the end of all our exploring

will be to arrive where we started

and know the place for the first time."

[T. S. Eliot]

Fear of making that phone call.

Fear of that interview, fear of that exam.

Fear of letting go.

Fear of falling in love.

Fear of feeling too much, fear of not feeling anything anymore.

Fear of disappointment, fear of making mistakes. Fear of regretting. Let's stop facing everything as if we were to the front. We are not risking our lives.

Always ask ourselves what we are really risking, and learn to distinguish between real risks and childhood fears that we carry with us. Not everything is dangerous, not today that you are an adult.To err is human. It teaches us to try new ways, to persevere, to smile at ourselves, not to abandon what we believe in.

Choosing our fears is choosing not to live. Everything has a risk, but it is a relative risk compared to ceasing to live and feel. And to take risks is to get excited, to feel the blood pulsing in your veins. We laugh, we cry, we make mistakes, we get, we learn, we lose, we get angry, we start over. Living is beautiful for this.

Drop the thought, and take your steps.

Action is the best antidote to paralyzing thought.

Breathe, you are alive.And nothing else matters.

Chapter VI
You and I

For our being there

For those we love

For our parents or children

For our work

For our passions, desires, and values.

For our dreams and the things we believe in.

Because if our every wound

it is a wound of love,

with love,

we will heal it.

One, Two, Three

The couple is the meeting of two units, not of two halves.

I believe that anyone who has left their parents' home to go their own way has experienced a massive change in their relationship with them.

It's a bit like leaving you really find you can love them.

Each individual first needs to identify himself, reach himself, to then enter into a love relationship.

Here, in the couple, it is the same.

A natural, almost mathematical order.

Before 1.

Then the 2.

And then the 3.

It is the perception of oneself as a complete individual (1) that allows us to live a healthy love relationship (1 + 1 = 2) and not the product of expectations, demands, emotional dependencies (it is not the other who must provide what's missing to achieve the unit!).

And it is only from two complete and identified units that something different can be born (3, something more than the sum of the parts. The—we—, a project, a new life).

Too often, we reverse this natural order.

And the sums, in the end, don't add up.

It will be difficult

As you slowly go away

To seek alone

What you will be

[A modo tuo, Ligabue]

There will be a moment when you will have to, despite yourself, let your child go his way.

So that he can become a man, an adult.

It will be difficult.

You will clash with your fears, but you will choose to face them, without discharging them on the other, to not let them hinder his path with feelings of guilt and victimhood.

It will be a gesture of true love.

The biggest you can ever make.

The real one; wanting the other—your child—to become what he wants to be.

Too often, we forget that all this also applies to our couple. Love is leaving the other free to be. Without hindering him and our path with victimization, expectations, and guilt.

Just so the love can be a choice of sharing and growth, and not a mortifying web of projections, fears, and addictions.

And remember, the other is not responsible for your history, your fears, and your frailties. Learn how to manage and deal with them.

Dumping it on him is an act of pure selfishness (if you really loved me, you wouldn't do it).

Adult love has come to terms with personal fears, leaving room for choice and the freedom to be oneself.

—Volo ut sis—I want you to be what you are. You.

The unique beauty of an imperfect Being.

Don't be afraid. Because people left free don't come back, they stay; they never left.

Humane, Too Humane

Love stories are not fairy tales.

They are in our imagination, in our expectations or projections, sometimes in our memories.

Love stories are human affairs.

And men are not mental concepts.

They are not ideas. They are not stories in books.

Men are reality and blood.

They are fears, insecurities, and asymmetries.

We lived it as children, the idea of an image; cartoon heroes, film actors. Mom and Dad, in their role as parents. Discovering them as a man and a woman was unsettling but liberating. They were human too, and they too were wrong.

Ignoring our human part means denying ourselves the reality of what we are.

The illusions support but then move away.

Ideals feed but then disappoint.

Your partner is human, imperfect but actual, just like you.

We grew up with the tales of eternal love.

We grew up with the illusion of two parents who would be together forever (and many did, to keep us believing it).

We grew up between romantic films, between love read, seen, photographed, told, imagined.

As if love were a magical powder that envelops you and never leaves you.

But love is instead a complex thing and ours.

It is the inflexible and inexplicable result of a range of factors: biochemistry, animal instinct, smell, interests and passions, projections and expectations, palpitations, and genes.

The imaginary and the concrete. The earth and the stars.

Love changes.

Love is transformed.

Love grows or fades.

Love ends.

The real miracle is to make it last. Going through the storms of continuous changes, of asymmetries, of boredom and contrasts, of profound acceptance, tolerance, balancing between shared spaces and our own, compromises between sharing and small secrets together.

Love is a complex thing.

A magical fairy tale, deeply humane.

An Hour, a Day, or a Lifetime

We believed that love was nurturing. Like a mother with her baby. But we were grown up, and then we realized that we were investing the partner with a role that does not belong to him and that it would not be right to make him play. He would have weakened us.

We believed that love was protection and guidance. Like a father with his son. But we had legs to move and the right to make mistakes and try again to find our way alone. And then we realized we wanted to be free to choose. To get dirty and fall, to get up, understand, try again.

We believed that love was suffering and lack. The romantic one of nineteenth-century novels and films. That of escapes and pursuits, that of tears and yearnings. But we had lips to smile, and we soon realized that love is instead possibility and presence. It is an addition and not a loss. It is one plus one and not the sum of two halves.

Finally, we arrived at a certainty.

As clear as water, as simple as air.

Love is being yourself. Without expectations, projections, overloads tied to one's existential knots. Without assigned roles, mother father, and novel together, in the spontaneous freedom of Being. Pure field, meeting of two individuals, single, who stand alone and decide to walk the stretch of road of their present together.

Choosing each other, every time.

An hour, a day, or a lifetime.

"I do my thing and you do your thing.

I am not in this world to live up to your expectations,

And you are not in this world to live up to mine.

You are you, and I am I, and if by chance we find each other, it's beautiful.

If not, it can't be helped."

[F. Perls]

Love is not controlling, not overpowering.

It is not wanting the other according to one's expectations.

Love is respect.

From the Latin—respicere—, to look.

Love is the ability to see a person as he is (not as we would like him to be), know his essence and individuality.

Love is wanting the other to be as it is.

Love is joy, not pain.

Love adds, does not take away.

Love is expansion, not contraction.

Love is openness and breath, not breathlessness.

Love is selection, not need.

Love is a gift, not a sacrifice.

Love is side by side, not above or below.

Love is life, not mortification.

Love is freedom, not control.

Love is Me—With—You, not Me—Why—You.

Love is an encounter.

But a genuine encounter is only possible between two individuals who know how to stand on their own legs.

To not let you run away

I locked the door and handed the key to you

["The console", T. Ferro and C. Consoli]

Other than elective affinities.

The truth is that you meet and fit in with each other's shadow areas.

More than a meeting of loving senses, the relationship is a marriage of neurosis.

And here is the real challenge. Growing up together is also embracing the other and his world, and not the other—second—oneself.

Or the relationship risks transforming itself into the scenario of a mortifying self—representation; the possibility for both to re-propose and perfect their own dysfunctional dynamics, their own patterns, and their own self-image.

Until the break.

Really being oneself.

There is no other way to meet and unite.

Because if you choke yourself out of fear of not being accepted, both of you will be paying the price.

The other may find someone more responsive to his needs, and you will find yourself dealing with the most atrocious of betrayals; towards yourself and your deepest values.

I am me, and no one else.

And if it is with me that you will be, then we will be the result of a real encounter; two people choosing each other.

Love is freedom and choice.

You have the key, you can go out whenever you want.

And I'll know that if you stay here, in this room where I am, it's because you want to be with me.

Control has nothing to do with love; it has to do with fear.

It is necessary to have reckoned with one's own shadows to meet in the light of Us.

Seven Seconds

Chapter VII
Of Water and Wind

The greatest waste in the world is the difference between what we are and what we could become.
[Ben Herbster]

It is fluidity and change that is natural. Like the seasons, day and night, growth and aging, the flow of rivers, and the continuous evolution of all.

Rigidity and attachment, on the other hand, are too often the result of resistance and fear. And they end up becoming the leading source of human suffering.

Panta rei, wrote Heraclitus, —everything flows—.

We decide whether to *flow with* or *flow against*.

Balance is not stillness. Balance is the result of continuous adjustments, changes, and progressive settlements.

Balance is the product of flexibility and the capacity inherent in nature and man to continuous adaptation.

That everything changes while you are experiencing it

and that some things barely align.

[Spostato di un secondo, M. Masini,]

It's the joints that screw us.

But this was born for our need to want to fit everything. Crushing our instances, our desires, in the illusion of giving us an accomplished shape. A sense. A role. An image. A social function. The answer to an expectation.

And so we suffer. We suffer if a story ends, we suffer if we fall in love, we suffer if we feel a desire —we shouldn't feel—, we suffer if things are not as they should be.

They raised us with the idea of form as a value. The stubborn adherence to oneself as a principle.

What a deception. The fear of the uncertain becomes the prison of a body that quivers like a pressure cooker.

Feeling wrong. Feeling we shouldn't.

"It's not fair, but I feel it."

There is only one truth. Everything changes, too.

We are people, not mathematical systems.

Forces in eternal becoming. Like water, capable of adapting to the container that houses it.

We are made of fragmentation, shadows, disasters, drives, and instincts.

Let yourself go, breathe your Now.

Stop defining yourself
And enjoy all the potential of Being
[A. Jodorowsky]

Be formless. Limitless, like water.
[B. Lee]

I meditated on how much our sufferings are linked to the conflict between form and content.

Think about it; we suffer from a relationship that no longer works because our desires are no longer what they used to be. Because we find ourselves enrolled in a faculty and now we would like to do something else. Because we want to leave our home or city.

We suffer because the form we attributed (or they have attributed) to us cannot contain the mutability of its content anymore.

And then we remain there, conflicting between the will and

the fear of changing and a worn and tight dress that now holds us and mortifies.

The truth is one: we are constantly changing.

And we should learn to continually adapt to a new form. It is not a question of striving; it is the natural evolution of Being.

We are born without limits, then, over the years, we harness ourselves in a pre-established form.

"That's how I am," we say, without realizing that this is how we devalue ourselves.

Panta rei. Everything flows.

Everything else is fear, social conventions, mortifying habits, the need for security that becomes, day after day, a cage that extinguishes our evolution and enthusiasms.

If we don't like where we are, we can move,

we are not trees

[Snoopy]

Stubborn consistency is an abomination of Being more than a virtue. The balance is in flexibility, not in rigid obstinacy.

Everything constantly changes in nature. The seasons, the night and the day, the clouds in the sky, the wind, the waves of the sea. Panta rei, wrote Heraclitus; everything flows.

Your desires, opinions, needs, passions, tastes, skin, relationships, clothes, home, gaze on the world change.

Truth is not a monolithic and immobile concept.

The truth also changes, transforms, it moves.

—Right— is what is good for you at a given moment of your Existence.

A matter of principle assumes as its founding basis—the principle—something that concerns a time now gone. An obstinate anachronism that has very little of the beginning and growth, and that too often ends only by decreeing the end of bonds, relationships, and the natural—and healthy— change of Being.

I should apologize to myself

for thinking I wasn't good enough

[A. Merini]

The end of a relationship is often the result of the emergence of desires and perspectives that exclude the partner. People change, and if they don't change together, the outcome is the relationship breakup.

Those who leave decide to take a new path, more suited to their current desires and perspectives.

Often those who are left make the mistake of feeling defective. Discarded. Not enough.

It is a mistake because it is not he or she who is —less—. It is the one who leaves to want —other—. Not —more—, people are not comparable. Simply something else.

Roads cross, people meet, walk the road together until they want the same things, but they may separate.

It is no one's fault, and no one can feel less than another.

And then, suddenly, she started to cry.

I looked at her, something more than seeing with her eyes, and maybe that was when I felt her.

It was no longer a dazzling cascade of words.

She was real. She was in contact with that pain. And me with her. That thread of tears identified us and united us as human beings. Me, you. Person to person.

We were together, we could really see each other, maybe for the first time. And no words were needed.

Never allow others to underestimate you.

This doesn't happen. It can't happen if you don't allow it.

Do not seek confirmation of who you are in a partner or in the eyes and gestures of others.

The awareness of who you are is the center of your Being. Everything else comes later. And remember.

You are worth what you know you are worth, not what someone else's opinion has established.

Look up, you are beautiful.

Nobody can be better than you.

Forget Yesterday, Start Today

So let's stop, there on the shore, watching the sea.

A slow and constant movement that calms and clears thoughts and anxieties.

Like an amniotic fluid.

A return to our point of origin.

The sea brings order.

The sea whispers. It does not speak.

It moves to the rhythm of our breathing, of our heartbeat.

Now, finally, slow.

Hypnotic, like the waves.

Let's give us the sea.

Let's give us the life we deserve.

Tomorrow is a mental construction that can become a trap.

"I will do it tomorrow."

"Will I make it tomorrow?"

Today is yesterday's tomorrow. It is that moment in time—the present—which contains in itself every possibility of action, choice, and change.

Procrastination is an alibi, a lack of responsibility. It is placing an action on a basis made of pure thought. Today you can choose, today you can do it. And then, if not now, when?

Chapter VIII
I Start Again from Myself

"Know Yourself"

In ancient Greek γνῶθι σαυτόν, gnōthi sautón; it was the inscription located in the temple of Apollo in Delphi, the—Oracle—.

A warning; before asking, before knowing and exploring the world, learn about yourself.

Before judging,

Before complaining,

Before condemning,

Before attacking,

Before claiming

First of all, before the other, place emphasis on You.

Yet we hardly do. It is much easier identifying causes and external enemies (by taking responsibility and weakening us) than questioning and starting from ourselves. Knowing yourself is the essential basis for relating healthily with others. It allows you to identify and recognize your share of responsibility in determining the situations we complain about. There are very few sufferings that, at least in part, we are not choosing and helping to maintain.

Would you ever accept living where you don't know about rooms, resources, and limits?

So come on, —nosce te ipsum—, know yourself.

It will be the beginning of an extraordinary adventure.

#Communicating?

I read that about 95% of the photos we take with smartphones will not be printed and will be lost due to breakdown/replacement of the same.

The thing is, we no longer take pictures for ourselves, to keep memories.

Today we take pictures mainly to post them on social networks. We take selfies to show where we are, what we do, how cool, beautiful, thin, happy we are.

And then, once this function is fulfilled, who cares if that photo will be lost.

We are all slaves to the approval of others.

But if between living our moments or publishing them, we choose this second option, we are devaluing ourselves.

It's like saying; your approval matters more than what I live.

To communicate. From the Latin—communicare—, to put in common, derived from—commune—, composed of cum, together, and munis, value, function.

Communication is a social expression, a putting a value in someone's service or putting something out of oneself.

What values are we putting at the service of others?

Public images and smiles clash with a private sphere often made of profound loneliness and incomprehension.

A profound disconnection between what we are and how we appear. Each mask takes us away from our true essence. Maybe it's time to hear, touch, smell, look into each other's eyes again.

Stop deceiving yourself.

Lift your eyes, and look.

Life is there, all around.

Half a meter higher of your fixed eyes on a mobile phone screen.

It Happened on This Day

I am not sure about the story of Facebook memories. I am not sure about the immediate availability of anyone and the carousel of photos of the events in real-time.

There is wisdom in our psyche.

As well as in our memories.

Often momentary forgetfulness is a functional process.

Functional to letting go of something or someone that is now beyond our life, to the energies to invest in new beginnings, to the subtle balance of our present, to the dignified respect for a time now gone.

We don't forget—by chance—, but because in a precise historical moment of our life, that memory is unnecessary or not functional to our Being.

I want to choose to forget.

I want to choose to temporarily put aside.

I want to choose to remember my teenage love as it was and not find a middle-aged woman in front of my eyes.

I want to trust my memories and my forgetfulness.

Balance of faces, events, names, confusion in motion, a silent and accomplice background of my Now.

I claim the right not to communicate.

I claim the right of withdrawal and silence.

I claim the right not to necessarily respond in the ways and times urgently imposed on me by an era of totalizing, draining, and often meaningless communication.

I claim the right not to experience the existence of smartphones, SMS, Facebook, and WhatsApp as a cage, but as a free choice.

After all, even in the days of the intercom, it could be denied. One look at the street through the curtains, and you pretended not to be home.

Communication is and must be a conscious choice by both parties.

A choice.

And every choice assumes accepting or refusing.

I claim the right to silence and my spaces.

It is not disrespect for you, but respect for me and my life.

There is an absolute truth in our existence.

Everything, everything changes.

Nothing stays the same.

And this also applies to pain.

However much you may suffer now, this pain will pass.

It will transform.

It is a certainty.

There will be a time when you will think back to today, and a smile will rise on your face.

It's a new day, a new today, a new you.

When night is almost done,

And sunrise grows so near

That we can touch the spaces,

It's time to smooth the hair

And get the dimples ready,

And wonder we could care

For that old faded midnight

That frightened but an hour.

[E. Dickinson]

The real voyage of discovery consists not in seeking new landscapes, but in having new eyes

[M. Proust]

Happiness is a state of fullness of one's Being and one's feeling.

It is a state of deep awareness, free from conditionings and blocks that affect our free flow.

It is to immerse yourself fully and confidently among the sinuous waves of life, fully experiencing all it offers.

Happiness.

It is laughing with all your smile and crying with all your tears.

When we were children, we lived worlds of infinite fullness. Do you remember? A stone was a moving train, a ball the world to chase. The fullness of the heart, the enthusiasm of doing.

A continuous —Now—.

No yesterday or tomorrow.

Happiness, as the fullness of immersion

in the experience of existing.

Then we grew up.

And that —Now— got impoverished every day. We have crushed it between the weight of the past we carry with us, and the fear of an unknown future.

We fooled ourselves, delegating our idea of happiness to something to be achieved. The degree, the love, the car, the house, the children. The goal, and no longer the process.

We believed we could solve our happiness as a mathematical equation. A ratio between today and yesterday, between how it was and how it is, between what we would like and when we have, between the lives of others and ours, between—if only I had…— and the reality of our days.

An equation that never comes back, a continually failing ratio.

We have made ourselves unhappy, moving that longed-for happiness into an elsewhere made of pure thought and therefore elusive.

Perhaps one day, we will understand that what we call happiness is nothing more than being truly in the reality of our day. A movement of the soul that nothing and no one can give us or take away from us.

It is ours, deeply ours.

It is in the smile of a stranger. In savoring a wedge of orange. In tucking the ones we love. In the thrill of discovery.

Whatever you do, do it with love. Do it fully. No yesterday or tomorrow.

There is still that child in the folds of your gestures and memories. He plays on the beach with a stone. He invents worlds. He doesn't define it, but he really lives what he will one day call happiness.

He is not out.

It is not what.

It is not when.

It is yourself. It is how. And it is Now.

No one is condemned or injured by their yesterday.

Although sometimes it is easier to think that than to take responsibility for one's days.

You can spend a lifetime kicking, getting angry, blaming outside of yourself.

This will not change things.

There is a strength in you that you cannot ignore.

—Resilience—.

That totally human ability to face difficult situations and to get back, always.

Whatever your past was,

what remains is your Now.

And maybe you can choose to give it the value it deserves because so many of the I can't are a choice. Yours.

Change your stars, today you can.

The present, your legs, and a road.

And the courage to go.

Try, dare, launch yourself, make a mistake, fall, get up, try again, live!

Everything that blocks you in a web of fears has the consistency of pure thought.

You built it, day after day, and day after day, you can choose to stop listening to it.

So come on, choose to live. One day you will think about it with a smile, and you will say that yes, it was worth it.

You did what was right with your life; you really lived it. The first and fundamental step of any evolution and change process is to stop blaming the outside (the situation, the partner, the parents, life) and take responsibility for one's way of being in the world.

It is not the fault of an inauspicious fate, of lack of affection, of abandonment.

Not anymore, not today.

Today it is my responsibility for how I am living.

Today it is my choice to take a different path.

It is about getting out of the—victim—position. Stop underestimating your power, face your fears, and embrace the path of possibility and change.

Before saying that others don't consider you enough, ask yourself how much value you are placing on yourself. You will find that there are no enemies to fight, except those you have created for yourself. It starts with you. It is the key to any change.

I stop complaining.

I am the operative part of my existence. It is my life, and I will do it as I wish.

Chapter IX
Cum-finis

Confines

"He put himself in the therapist's hands."

A phrase that has been heard several times, a simple expression that hides a psychic prerequisite that is likely to become a disempowering and discouraging attitude.

Putting oneself in someone's hands is the surrender of one's freedom and power. To do, to choose, to decide. It may make sense for a 4-year-old who does not yet have the tools and the potential to survive and understand the demands of him. But not for an adult. An adult has every resource in him to cope with life events. To change, grow, choose, decide. Potentials that are sometimes overshadowed by influences, psychic residues of the past, ancient fears, now out of date or exasperated.

And instead, regaining one's freedom is precisely one of the ultimate goals of therapy.

Every therapeutic success is the outcome of synergy, of a good meeting between the therapist—with his presence, humanity, empathy, and competence—and the patient—with their own motivation and their own desire to change and get involved. But in this synergy, what must always be valued is the person's responsibility (from respondere: to respond), as the ability to respond adequately and adultly to events. Ability to choose. To change, or not to (but consciously).

A therapist does not hold the lives of his patients in his hands. A therapist is *with* the person who turns to him to help him become aware that he has a hand. That shaking it to grasp his goals and change or opening it to let go of someone or something is a choice that can and should be wholly his.

The true self is what you are,

not what they made of you.

[P. Coelho]

Have you ever thought about how our roles cause conflict and suffering?

The role of mother, father, wife, lover, worker, friend.

A dress was worn for a deep need for self-confidence and identification that becomes tight and uncomfortable.

And then life takes care of breaking the banks.

It does not allow itself to be limited.

The truth is, we are never all one way. Shadows and shades are an integral part of our being in the world. No dress can ever contain the extraordinary variability of ours.

To be.

To limit or abandon oneself.

To hold back or to let go.

The self-confidence or the emotion of the moment.

"How much happiness do we give up for our need for security?" wrote Galimberti.

Suppressing one's emotions means giving up the most vital part of our existence.

Maybe we are afraid of feeling truly free.

Charlie Brown, "Do you ever think about the future, Linus?"
Linus, "Oh, yes. Always"
Charlie Brown, "How do you think you want to be when you grow up?"
Linus, "Shamefully happy!"
[C. M. Schultz]

It is a mistake to call happiness—in absence—. "I'll be happy when I get... when I'm rid of... when things are."

In this way, we delay our happiness, relegating it to a time that is to come. Or we attribute it to an old-time gone, an idealized time that, in our memory, appears in a sectorial way (perhaps even then we were complaining about something!). Who pays the cost is our Now, the only temporal space that has in itself the seeds of every possibility of being and every change.

That's life. Ups and downs. We laugh, we cry, we get scared and angry, we are amazed, we discover and overcome, we fail, and we try again. No one is immune from it, and life is surprising and beautiful precisely in its fullness.

Do not make the mistake of imagining happiness as a state of beatitude in which nothing happens. It would be the same as not living anymore.

Bliss is of the saints. We are given to live as human beings.

The earthly wonder of desires, conflicts, changes, enthusiasms, disappointments, senses, thoughts, emotions.

Hope to experience them all.

Every nuance of being.

It will mean that you lived your life.

Really.

Laugh with all your smiles, cry with all your tears.

Identical and Different

I love fragments, the insignificant little things, the missing parts, the disruptions.

They are the movement and soul of our being.

I love the unconventional, the unscheduled, the subtle amazement of the unexpected.

It's growth every time you meet them.

I love frailties, moved eyes, insecurities, broken words, hesitations.

They remind me that no matter who you are, where you come from, or how you are made. We are human, you and I. I can hear and recognize you.

Strong and fragile, identical and different.

Divided by a thousand days and a whole life but together, partners and united, in this unique and beautiful moment of our existence.

I work with people.

The real ones, the ones that too often we hide, between pleasantries and a thread of embarrassing fear.

I work with emotions.

Those underneath, those suffocated, those stuck between tightened lips and stomach pains.

It is both reassuring and disturbing.

It destabilizes discovering that we are also something else. Never white or black, but unique palettes of infinite shades of gray. Changeable, inconsistent, sometimes liars, frightened, imperfect, and therefore beautiful.

It reassures the universality of our pains. We all suffer for love.

For the one denied by distant parents, for the lost one, for the one dreamed of, trampled on, pursued, idealized.

And it is love that hurts, and it is love that heals.

I work with people.

I know the infinite beauty of our fragility.

I know the infinite sense of closeness in crossing two eyes that look up after a cry in the silence. Naked souls, never contact was more intimate.

I know that winters give way to springs.

That it is possible to put the pieces of a life back together, one step at a time.

Turn the page, let go, start over.

I know for sure that no matter how much rain you went through, there is always the first ray of a new serene.

Still and always, on my feet again.

Because the night will not extinguish the day, and—*too late*—is only authentic when your heart has beaten its last beat.

Do not do to the other what he would not want to be done to him.

[V. Magrelli]

Self-centering is one of the main reasons for discord, resentment, misunderstanding, and missed encounters; wanting and perceiving the world and others according to one's perspective.

As Watzlawick said, nothing is more dangerous than the illusion that there is only one reality, one's own.

Really understanding the other, and respecting him, requires something more than his simple evaluation within one's own perceptual and value schemes. It is right/wrong are concepts that can only be evaluated in the reference system of those experiencing something.

The other is, in fact, another.

Another story, other experiences, other parents.

Really seeing it, respecting it, understanding it, and feeling it, is an act of humility and decentralization. I get what you are experiencing because I can feel it as *you* are feeling it.

Or it all comes down to a mortifying and ephemeral self-confirmation of one's rigid evaluation schemes.

This is how we meet. This is how we enrich ourselves with reciprocal exchange.

People often don't have clear emotions.

Not to mention the ideas.

[Anonymous]

Emotions are all vital and functional.

Although we commonly divide them into —good— and —bad—, in reality, they all have a fundamental purpose; to guarantee our survival and good social interactions.

However, there may be the tendency to mask some emotions, such as sadness, because considered improper or not allowed in the individual's family and educational history.

It is in these cases that we use what is called parasitic emotion. Pretty frequently, for example, is the replacement of sadness, considered a negative and passive emotion, with anger, considered more active and desirable. But sadness has the fundamental function of putting us in touch with ourselves and with the need for change, as well as the social function of bringing others closer empathically, obtaining support and affinity. Anger, on the other hand, has the function of delimiting social spaces. It is a clear message not to override one's personal space and to re-establish limits and boundaries.

The outcome of this replacement is, of course, a real mess. An extreme distancing from one's true feeling and an enormous relational confusion.

Showing your emotions for what they are is not a sign of weakness.

True strength is knowing how to Be, here, now, with the emotion I feel.

And close my eyes to stop

something that

it's inside me [...].

You can't understand, if you want, call them

Emotions

[L. Battisti]

Oh, if I could picture myself

a single color that I have never seen

[S. Weöres]

Do you know that colors, in reality, do not exist?

We perceive colors based on the wavelengths refraction of light on objects. Our eyes are made to perceive *those* wavelengths and not others.

Other animals perceive infrared, which actually exists, but we don't see it, so we think it doesn't exist.

Almost all animals perceive in monochrome, and that is the world for them.

Insects perceive yellow and its shades, so they live in a world made of flowers. And that's their world.

The fact is that the world is not good or bad.

The world is how you want it, how you perceive it.

If I light the lamp of beauty, there will be beauty in the world
[A. Jodorowsky]

So let's stop trying to explain everything because the search for meaning risks making us lose the meaning itself of our existence.

The search for meaning is like the search for a frame in which to hang our beautiful picture. But life is not a painting. It is the movement of the brush on a white canvas instead.

Life is not the goal, it is not the home, it is not the wealth, it is not the conquest.

Life is all you do *during*.

And if there really is a meaning in our life, it is simply living it. Really.

So come on, let's have fun.

Let's experiment, let's get involved, let's get out of these patterns that too often turn into cages.

It's a great thing when you discover the possibility of being amazed.

Always.

Life is one, but the possibilities are many.

Let's take them back.

So grow up, but not too much.

Grow up just enough for you to have courage, to stop depending, to become independent and responsible for your life.

But grow just enough that you need to not stop dreaming, marveling, playing.

Grow up, but keep your inner child alive.

It will be the strength of your love, the enthusiasm of your hours, the curiosity of your discovery, the exciting thrill of your couple, the light and the beauty of your pure eyes, wide open to the world.

(...)For this reason, passion indicates in its most common sense a desire, a transport of the soul than thought has always contrasted with λόγος (logos), with reason, like the two polarizing forces of man.
[Italian dictionary]

Passions save you, always.

Whether it's a good book, a pen and a notebook, your legs, your gaze on the world and a reflex camera, the black and white frets, the strings of a guitar, a fishing rod, the movement of your body, and your breath.

The beauty of passions is that they are self-responsible. They just depend on you.

They are something that always follows you, whether you are in a room, on the street, in a hospital bed, or on the seashore.

Nothing and no one can take them away from you.

They never, never leave you alone, and never bored.

Passions save you, always.

Alice, "How long is forever?"

White Rabbit, "Sometimes, just one second".

[L. Carrol]

It is the most precious thing we have, and so often, we forget it. It is not the money, it is not the objects we own, it is not our clothes, our car, or our house.

It is the *time*.

Everything we buy, we do not with money (which are simple pieces of paper chosen as a unit of exchange) but with the time it took us to work and earn it.

Yet, we overestimate money and devalue our time.

Our time is the only thing that never goes back.

Our time is limited, and we can't buy more.

So often, it is at the end of our days that we realize this. We would then be willing to do anything to go back and have more.

The time.

We always ask ourselves how we are spending our time.

Are we giving it the correct value, or are we mortifying it, always postponing our desires to a future time?

Living is now.

This moment, this time. It is all we have.

Our most precious asset.

The treasure is at the end of the rainbow

and finding it near, in your bed,

likes it much less.

[Il negozio di antiquariato, N. Fabi]

It seems that everyone is chasing something far away.

Everyone seems to want what they don't have, no longer have, or don't have yet.

It seems that everyone is absorbed in the reality of their days and with desires in an indefinite elsewhere.

It seems that everyone is not really present to what they experience when they experience it. And so I am single. I do not look at the freedom of my Being but the lack of a partner.

And so I'm in a couple. I don't look at the poetry of sharing but at the lost freedom of being single.

ut let's not confuse reality with ideas. They belong to different orders, and therefore not comparable. The first belongs to the tangible, the second to pure thought.

Dreaming is easy.

Finding the magic in the reality of one's day is the real achievement.

Smile at your Now.

You are single, and you miss a partner. Someone to share with. Evenings at home on the sofa.

You are in a couple, and you miss freedom. Going out with friends. The evenings in the pubs.

You work, and you miss free time.

You have too much free time, and you would like to work.

You are young, and you want to grow up to do adult things.

You are an adult, and you would like to go back to do young people's things.

You are in your city, but you would like to live elsewhere.

You are elsewhere, but you would like to come back to your city.

Maybe it's time to stop looking at what we miss and start living in the present, truly appreciating what we have.

Enjoy the scent of your home before looking for the ones in the world.

Because nothing is taken for granted, and everything is a gift.

Give it value.

Babies grab their feet with their hands and bring them to their mouths.

In an extreme closeness between desires and steps.

The adult, on the other hand, has feet far apart, not easy to grasp.

Between a desire and a step, there is the distance of a whole body.

Between a desire and a step, there is the distance of a whole body.

Because someday, if there is a showdown in this life, it will certainly not be the praise of your parents and friends, or pats on the back, or prizes and gifts to attest to how good you have been.

Good boy. What is it, then? What does everyone expect from you?

And no.

Because someday, if there is a showdown in this life, it will be a reminder of what you have done. They will be images and smiles. They will be your follies, your secrets, those stolen moments, the balancing act of every day between your different roles.

You will have truly lived following your values and not those attributed to you, to the best of what you can. You will think about it with a smile, a hint of melancholy, and you will have no regrets.

Now you are, today you exist.

Take a step, let yourself go to your life.

Everything needs to change

so that everything remains as it is

[G. Tomasi di Lampedusa]

And let's remember that people change, even our partners.

Let's stop relating today to a time gone by. That time is, in fact, gone. Today is a new time.

The art of loving each other will never deny or curse change but welcome it and adapt every moment to a new being.

Only in this way will we be able to discover and choose each other every day.

Not motionless photographs in the swamps of the past, but flying birds towards the green expanses of tomorrow.

"It's Not Easy"

If you scroll through the pages of your life in your mind, the answers you give yourself, the words you speak, you will often find this comment.

It is not easy.

It is not easy to change.

It is not easy to choose.

It is not easy to forgive.

It is not easy to accept.

And the last, very powerful, it is not easy to live.

Maybe we should realize that this is a way to trick us and put ourselves in the passive position of someone who can't do anything (but can complain).

It's not easy, sure, but it's definitely possible if you really want to.

It is not easy to remain in the same situation for a lifetime.

It is also not easy to be unhappy all the time.

It is also not easy to always be angry with someone again and again.

But to say that life is difficult is an abomination.

Life isn't good or bad, easy or hard.

Life simply *is*.

It's how we choose to live it.

We make it one way or another.

We fight and kick on nonexistent battlefields too often.

There is no struggle,

there is no land, no conquest.

Too many times, it is enough to let go of what happens to get back to breathing.

Acceptance is this, being in what it is, without forcing.

To live with and not against.

May it be blessed

As absurd and complex it seems to us,

Life is perfect

And we should learn

To hold it tight

[Fiorella Mannoia]

"We were the right people at the wrong time."

Nothing could be more false.

There are no right people or wrong times.

People exist in the continuous evolution and transformation of their existence.

There is time, not right or wrong, but what you live in this moment. There is no middle ground; we will meet right now or each one on his own way.

Every moment is the right one.

And every real encounter is the result of a joint or—it is not—

.

It is useless to torment oneself in digressions among the unfathomable scenarios of lost possibilities.

It wasn't the wrong time.

It simply wasn't and couldn't be.

Failure does not exist.

It does not exist in any animal species, in any natural event.

Failure is a purely human invention.

It is the name we give when things don't match our expectations or when we leave because we are tired of trying again. Life and events are simply—neither good nor bad and not necessarily as in our expectations—and must be accepted in their natural flow.

There is no such thing as failure.

There are initiatives, attempts. There is adjusting to new stimuli. There is letting go, as an act of true love, for others or oneself. Nothing is more terrible than not starting, not trying, not believing it. It would be like not living. It is never a failure; it is always an experience.

"If You Are Nice, I Love You"

And so we grow up with the profound idea of having to do things for each other to be recognized and appreciated.

But no man or woman will love you for what you do.

They will love you because you have elements in you that will resonate with the world of the other.

They will love you because you are so; unique and unrepeatable in the naturalness of who you are.

Love has nothing to do with doing, it has to do with being.
[A. Lommatzsch, FISIG conference, 2017, Catania]

Don't give in to the mortifying self—deception of wanting to look different than you are. Everything has the right to be, and everyone has the right to love and be loved for what they really are. No nature can be hidden in the long run.

A drop carves the mountain, and a flower grows even among the driest rocks.

Because Being yourself will never stop making mistakes. Rather. Being yourself will mean giving yourself permission to make mistakes.

Free to make mistakes, free to choose.

"Home Is Where You Are"

Perhaps you have already thought about dedicating it to the person you love.

But stop for a moment.

Try to dedicate it to you.

Yes, to yourself.

And make—home—the center of your being, your breath.

A comfortable place.

Wherever you are, alone or in the company, on a deserted beach or in city traffic.

Home is where you are.

First of all, before any—we—, there is—me—.

Only in this way can an encounter be a real encounter. And not the fruitless and mortifying web of projections, addictions, and expectations.

I open my home to you, and you are not—my home—.

I will not be homeless because I have mine.

And when the door closes, the warmth of my walls remains to lull in my breath.

Still and always, with me.

"Truth Is Protection"

An absolute, cryptic, lapidary phrase.

My therapist and teacher, Antonio Ferrara, often repeated it.

At that time, I did not fully grasp the meaning. I thought, "but are not the little lies we tell ourselves and others that protect us?" Today I understand what he meant.

The web of lies we tell to ourselves and others, rather than protect us, ends up harnessing us in a mess of mortifying stasis; the illusion of protection becomes a lack of evolution. No risk, no jolt, no development.

There is only one form of protection: truth. Truth towards oneself, towards one's intentions, values, goals, aspirations.

The leap into the void of transparency is in itself its safety net.

Here I am, I am this, exactly like that.

And I'm no longer afraid of being myself.

I will love the other in you, not my projections of what you should be to me.

You are not an extension of my wishes, nor will I be for you.

To love you is to really see you, your being different than me that becomes wealth and growth. Not my expectations, not my gaps to fill, nor despair to cure.

I want you to be who you are.

I, you, and a shared space that becomes the fertile ground for —We—.

Sometimes it is necessary to move away to find the correct closeness.
Sometimes it is necessary to stop to really start.
Sometimes it is necessary to let go to find.

What If Leaving Meant Going Back?

We identify—home—with what we know, but isn't it true that feeling at home is feeling fully present to oneself?

Think of the journey, the discovery, the senses, and that amazed gaze. To small fears, new adaptations, experiments, and new paths.

Maybe leaving is really going back.

Perhaps leaving is actually finding.

Away from old habits, from worn-out relationships, from the house where one was born, from the convictions, and from known habits.

Embrace the fullness of self.

Raise the anchor, take the first step.

Leaving to go back to oneself.

Do you know what the problem is?

In the end, you discover that too many things are different from how they have been told.

You realize only by living that life is full of infinite disasters.

Nothing seems to follow the reassuring patterns in which you grew up. Not everything fits together. Almost nothing is linear. Your lifetimes are not.

Your body is not concerning the years you feel.

Your parents aren't.

Your relationship is not.

Your wishes are not.

Your growing children are not.

Your days are not, nor your moods.

If you think about it, it is not that negative. Rather. It makes living something like an extraordinary adventure, a continuous discovery.

You spend too much time complaining about disruptions and looking at those badly overlapping edges rather than trying new forms, adapting to new combinations of being, and discovering new parts of yourself. But so you lose everything.

For example, to keep hitting your head against a wall instead of jumping, grabbing the edge, pulling yourself up with your arms, and finding out what's beyond.

And, trust me, there is always something beyond.

Feeling, Not Thinking

Thinking is one of our functions, as are intuition and emotion.

We overlook the latter and overestimate the former too often.

But overthinking can also block you.

And, trust me, so much of our being is meant to be lived, not thought of or explained.

Abandon yourself. Dare. Try. Listen.

May the experience be the guide, not your thinking.

A great discovery I made was to realize that there was no single way of being in the world. What my parents taught me, or what I saw proposed on TV, from the people around, from the social context in which I grew up.

No. It was a lie, a gigantic lie.

I took for granted and immovable what was not taken for granted at all, just because it was proposed to me.

I realized that too many fears were totally unfounded (judgment, good image, other people's expectations, thirst for consideration), and things were absolutely relative.

I understood that my life could be guided by a few fundamental criteria:

Feeling good.

Really feeling me.

Doing the things I enjoyed doing.

So I stopped taking everything so seriously and started living my life with a smile. With the eyes of the child, I had been. Like a big, surprising game.

And I felt light.

25th December

Stop tonight.

Between one course and another, between a pandoro and a toast.

Stop.

Stop to observe the faces of your diners.

Stop and feel your breath and the taste of the foods you will eat.

Hear the voices, the emotions, the stories, and the smiles.

Feel the silences.

Feel the joy in the eyes of the little ones when they unwrap the gifts, hear the transmissions all the same with the background of Christmas songs.

Feel your grandmother if you're lucky enough to still have her there with you.

Feel your parents, their gestures (that are a bit yours), and that thread of continuity that unites you to their story.

Feel your children, the smile of tomorrow, and the persistence of memories.

Feel, feel everything.

Feel your life.

May it be a Christmas with the gift of time.

Yes, time. A time truly lived in the awareness of your center and your desires.

Because nothing is the same as today, and every moment lasts as long as a sigh.

Live it.

Breathe. You are here and now.

And that's all that matters.

"Eternal sunshine of the spotless mind"
[A. Pope]

Nature does everything according to the criteria of the economy. An underground water source finds a way to flow and turn into a stream, waterfall, river, down to the sea. Every curve, every deviation, every jump is not accidental; it is the way—the best one—to get where you should.

Instead, in human affairs, there is a paradoxical tendency towards complexity: immeasurable fears, hesitations, blocks linked to roles, social conventions, the expectations of others, an overestimation of the past and its residues or of the future and its consequences, often at the expense of a present crushed and mortified by the paralysis of every action.

And so, we make our way, not the simplest, but the most tortuous and labyrinthine. Many things, without the psychic residues we carry with us, would be more spontaneous.

Perhaps we should rediscover the natural grace of simplicity.

The beauty of a gesture, the warmth of a hug, the amazement of a candid wonder in this splendid adventure of existence.

Without past or future. Today, in all our full beauty.

You complain, what are you complaining about?
Grab a stick and pull out your teeth
[Malarazza, Roy Paci and Aretuska]

Complaint and victimhood are typical positions of the child's ego state. A passive position of someone who expects things to change with an intervention—from the outside—(like a child with his mother).

Beyond the manipulative, dependent, and potentially destructive nuances that a position of this type activates within adult relationships, a total self-depreciation is implicit in it; that of one's power, action, and freedom of choice.

Today you are an adult. Today it is no longer mom or dad's fault, the little friend who hurt you, or the circumstances. Too comfortable, as well as perfectly useless.

Today it is your freedom to choose, change your path, decide about your life.

Stop crying, stop moaning.

Move your steps, refresh the soul.

Because at the end of this long journey, what remains will be how you lived it.

That Now, which you looked casually, mortified in the memory of the past, or crushed each day in a frantic race to reach your tomorrow.

You have run a lot, you have not stopped, and what remains is the dust of a time had then, and today it cannot return.

Because we are given a time, this present, assigned to you when you wake up with no guarantees of your tomorrow.

Your time is not infinite.

It's up to you to give it the value it deserves.

Stop.
Breathe.
Live this moment with all of yourself.

In a few years, you will turn around and remember it with regret.

You almost did not notice it, so lost in the search for a continuous elsewhere.

You will close your eyes, and a sigh will slowly lift your chest.

And then you will give it a name.

You will call it happiness.

Live now. That's all that matters.

Seven Seconds

Chapter X
And I smile at My Now

We grew up hearing that what matters is studying, working, having a social position, earning money, getting married, and having children.

And many of us did it in an obstacle race against time that guaranteed us only stress and a good handful of years that have flown by.

Someone did it. Someone else didn't.

But we all found ourselves dealing with a sensation. Something we couldn't explain. A sense of widespread bewilderment, a vague confusion, an emptiness.

A whole colossal lie.

No one told us that what really mattered is that we were happy. Not a universal concept, not *their* happiness, but whatever happiness meant to *us*.

Doing what we like to do.

Carving out a time only ours.

Knowing and discovering, and then being able to choose.

Having the right to make mistakes, too.

Living according to our times and our ways. To love and be loved for who we are and not for what they wanted us to be.

To stop frantically chasing a pattern and paint the outline of our smile with our hands. The most important thing you can do with the time you are given is one; live it in a way that makes you happy.

But do you really believe that living is just working, producing, reaching goals?

Life is not a race, my friend.

There is no podium other than your conscience and a time that will never return.

Living is the way, not the goal.

Live this moment.

Yes, that's it, you spend reading this post. Living is what you will do next. Leaving the house, sleeping, being angry or forgiving, making that phone call you've been postponing for a long time, taking the bike, diving into the water from up there, caressing your grandmother's face.

This is living.

To live is to dedicate time to your passions and to the things you love. To live is to share with whoever you want, to laugh and cry together. To live is to learn to play an instrument, take dance lessons, devote yourself to a sport. To live is to leave for that place you've always seen on TV and discover what it smells like. To live is walking while breathing the grass. To live is the sunset and the stars on your head at night, on the beach.

To live is to turn the page, to smile at your changing body, to discover that you are still amazed, and you still have those fears, but today they almost make you smile. To live is to fall in love, again and again.

To live is the summer heat, it is the nights while it is cold and rain outside, it is the lost keys and the friends found, the old photos and the new books.

Living is a crazy adventure, my friend.

And you are the director and actor.

Because one day, when the curtain falls, all of this will be with you. In images and memories, in the stories of those who love you, in the gestures of your child, in the world that you made a better place.

That's life. This, yours, the only one you have.

Clench your fists and grab it before she slips away.

I Choose to Be

I choose to be.

I choose to learn something new.

I choose to devote myself to a hobby with the same passion as a child playing with a rubber ball.

I choose to delete the—if I had—, the—how it would have been—, the—if only—.

I choose to embrace my past to the extent that it has made me who I am. I let go of everything else; I don't need it.

I choose to stop draining my energy by regretting and to look at my today with confidence and respect.

I choose to stop distressing myself with unnecessary anticipatory anxieties for a future that, fortunately, I cannot know. Today I am, and that's all that matters.

I choose to let those I love free, aware that it is the only possible way to truly love someone.

I choose to face my fears instead of unloading them on those around me; they are not responsible for them.

I choose to let go of whoever wants to go. This is also love.

I choose to look my parents in the eye and see them as people, not a role. I choose gratitude; if I am here, it is thanks to them.

I choose to smile at my mistakes and not be distressed by the opinions of others. We are human beings; perfection does not belong to us.

I choose to try rather than let myself be blocked by stupid fears. And I choose to try again if I fail.

Satisfaction is gained in small steps.

I choose to forgive and to stop tormenting myself with unnecessary resentments.

I choose to value myself. And to give it to my time, knowing that it is my most precious asset. It is my life, the only one I have, and I will do it as I wish.

I choose to know myself, to discover and amaze myself every day.

I choose to experiment, always. A new road, a new food, a new book, a new look at what I don't know and what I think I know, but I'm wrong.

I choose doubts more than certainties.

I choose bare feet and fewer shoes.

I choose authenticity and abandon the useless masks. I can't please everyone, and that's okay.

I choose respect for my values.

I choose the commitment but also the leisure.

I choose a time to laugh, to share, but also a time for me, for silence, and for feeling myself.

I choose me, first of all.

I choose to be.

Here and now.

Now, and every moment of my days.

How stupid we are;

how many rejected invitations, how many unspoken words,

how many unrequited looks.

Sometimes life flows in front of us

and we don't even notice it.

["The Ignorant Fairies", by F. Ozpetek]

How much life spent chasing—the right thing—, trying to fit everything, pigeonholing and mortifying one's own requests in the name of a shape, a role, what others expect. The partner, the parents, the friends, the society. Pieces of life and us, crushed and annihilated in the name of stubborn consistency. The form, more than the substance.

How many unnecessary feelings of guilt, how many repressed emotions, how many gestures forgotten in the ocean of—if I had...?—.

If there is a hell, it is this; to become strangers to oneself.

Only to realize that the Great Judge does not arrive. It does not exist, except within us. There is no podium, no medal, no recognition, or handshake.

What exists is instead the end of your time, your last breaths.

If there can be a—never again—, this is it.

The last moments, and those accounts to do with oneself; how did I live my life?

The irreconcilable torment of—wish I had done it—. And the desire to want to give everything to go back and follow new paths.
But it is a thought that melts over time, in the silence of the last breath.

But today, you are. You exist and breathe.

Well, man!

Make that phone call.

Feed that talent.

Hug that person.

Say that—I love you—muffled in the silence of the heart.

Make love, go ahead and fuck, in any way you want.

Forgive.

Caress your parents' face. Thank them, they did what they could.

Live in all shades of your Being. You are not wrong. You are alive.

The hourglass is next door. The sand flows relentlessly, and it is not known for how long. Look at it, caress it.

Time is not your enemy but the engine of your days.

Close your eyes and breathe.

You exist.

Now reopen them, and live your moment.

www.ingramcontent.com/pod-product-compliance
Lightning Source LLC
Chambersburg PA
CBHW030257030426
42336CB00009B/418